Do Purpose

Why brands with a purpose
do better and matter more

David Hieatt

To Clare, Stella and Tessa

Published by
The Do Book Company 2014
Works in Progress Publishing Ltd
thedobook.co

Text © David Hieatt 2014
Illustrations © Olaf Ladousse 2014
Photography © Andrew Paynter 2014

The right of David Hieatt to be identified
as author of this work has been asserted
by him in accordance with the Copyright,
Designs and Patents Act 1988

To find out more about our
company, books and authors,
please visit **thedobook.co**
or follow us on Twitter **@dobookco**

5% of our proceeds from
the sale of this book is given to
The Do Lectures to help it achieve
its aim of making positive change
www.dolectures.com

Cover designed by James Victore
Book designed by Nick Hand

Printed and bound in Wales
by Gomer Press on Munken,
an FSC-certified paper
supplied by GF Smith

A CIP catalogue record for this book
is available from the British Library

ISBN 978-1-907974-13-7
3 5 7 9 10 8 6 4 2

Contents

FIND
YOUR
LOVE

For me, the most important brands in the world make you feel something. They do that because they have something they want to change. And as customers, we want to be part of that change.

These companies feel human. The founders tell us how the world could be. They bare their soul to us.

These companies have a reason to exist over and above just to make a profit: They have a purpose.

Yes, we admire the product they make. But the thing we love the most about them is the change they are making.

We love purpose-driven brands.

SANE PEOPLE QUIT

Starting a business is hard. You'll work like a crazy thing and have to sustain that over a long period of time. Poor pay. Terrible hours. Tons of stress. Any normal, rational person would quit. And that's what happens. When things get tough, and there will be a point when they do, sane people quit.

But purpose-driven entrepreneurs are different. They fall in love with the change they are making, so have to find a way to make it work. Their love stops them quitting. Love makes them persevere.

Love blinkers them to all the worry and stress. And it's their purpose that fuels that love.

CHAPTER ONE

PURPOSE

DRAW THREE CIRCLES

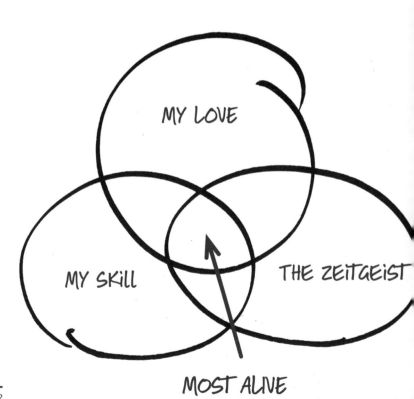

MY LOVE

MY SKILL

THE ZEITGEIST

MOST ALIVE

Here's an exercise to help find your purpose. First, draw three circles.

In the first circle write what you love doing; in the second circle write your skill; and in the third one write what the zeitgeist is.

Where these three circles overlap is where you're most alive. If I were you, I would start a company that lives in this intersection too. Because the chances of success are greater there. The chances of it making real change are greater. And the chance of it being more fun are greater there too.

My Love: Does it matter to you? Have you shown an interest in it from an early age?

My Skill: What is it I am good at? And will this startup use my skills fully?

The Zeitgeist*: What have you seen before all the others?

*A trend is the latest fashion, but it may just fade away.

A zeitgeist is a shift that will stay shifted.

TWO KINDS OF PASSION

IT'S IMPORTANT TO KNOW WHICH IS WHICH

I think it's helpful to understand passion. Because purpose-driven companies are mostly built with it.

I believe there are two types of passion. One is 'hot passion'. It is all heart; the head is not being called upon to think. And that means sometimes things can go wrong. Hot passion is a bit like infatuation – it burns brightly, but fades quickly.

Whereas 'cold passion' is calm, considered and long lasting. Both the brain and the heart are working together. Emotions have been taken out of decision-making. And decisions are given time, looked at from all angles. Cold passion is much more effective at getting results. Cold passion is like a lifelong love. Once decided upon, it's almost impossible to stop loving.

It's good to be aware of the difference between the two. To be successful, you will need to learn the art of cold passion. You will need to create a discipline where head and heart can both be involved in the decisions that you make. Taking the emotion out of something you feel very passionate about is far from easy. But easy don't build great.

DEFINE THE CHANGE THAT YOU WILL MAKE

RESPONSIBILITY FOR THE TOTAL

'What we take, how and what we make, what we waste, is in fact a question of ethics. We have an unlimited responsibility for the total. A responsibility which we try to take, but do not always succeed in. One part of this responsibility is the quality of the products and how many years the product will maintain its durability. To make a high-quality product is a way to pay respect and responsibility to the customer and the user of the product. A high-quality product, in the hands of those who have learned how to use it and how to look after it, will very likely be more durable. This is good for the owner, the user. But this is good as well as part of a greater whole: increased durability means that we take less (decreased consumption of material and energy), that we need to produce less (gives us more time to do other things we think are important or enjoyable), destroy less (less waste).'

This is the first page from a user manual from an axe company called Gransfors. They know why they are in business: To make axes that last. They want to change a society that thinks throwing away stuff is OK.

Extract reproduced by kind permission of Daniel Brånby, owner, Gränsfors Bruk.

It doesn't have to be another company. Maybe you need a bigger enemy than just another brand. It can be bad design. It can be time. It can be pollution. It can be ugliness. It can be bad service. It can be landfill. It can be complexity.

This will be your driver so pick your enemy well. This will become your purpose. Your fuel when you're tired out. Your reason to keep going when others call it a day. It will be why your customer prefers you over all the others. This is your purpose. The thing that separates you from all the others.

The companies that you love today started out with no more money than others, they just had more energy*. Their energy came from how much they wanted to change things. They knew well from day one what their enemy was.

What is your enemy?

*Purpose is the multiplier of energy.

DEFINE YOUR ENEMY

THE COMPETITION HAVE MORE OF EVERYTHING THAN YOU

More staff. More history. More distribution. More patents. More sales. More infrastructure. More contacts. More marketing. More money. (And they can raise plenty more.)

More followers on Instagram, Facebook, Twitter, Pinterest, Medium and Google Plus than you. They spend more on R&D than you turn over as a company. Their coffee budget is bigger than your marketing budget. They never run out of staples, they always have enough photocopier paper, their CEO doesn't have to put the bins out as well as lead the company.

Who would be crazy enough to try and take on a Goliath?

THE COMPETITION HAVE MORE OF EVERYTHING THAN YOU

More meetings. More committees. More red tape. More politics. More internal fighting. More rules. More regulations. More ideas being killed by research than you.

More out-dated business models. More de-motivated staff than you. More people wondering 'What is this company all about?' than you.

And then there is their legal department: The graveyard of humour, and anything else vaguely interesting or pioneering. Who cares if they never run out of staples or photocopier paper? There has never been a better time to be a small company. Don't worry about what they have. You have it all. You have something you want to change.

Brand X

They have customers. They have the past. They have an old business model. They're a commodity. They have to be cheaper. They are the status quo. In recessions, their customers leave and go to the cheapest. They have changed very little and can't remember why they started.

Brand Why

They have fans. They have the future. They
have a new business model. They are special.
They can charge a premium. They are respected.
Their fans love them. They are proud of them.
In recessions, their fans stick with them. They
are changing what they set out to.

YOU CAN'T WONDERFUL PASSING ALRIGHT.

GET TO
WITHOUT
THROUGH
BILL WITHERS

CALL YOUR HEROES

THEY HAVE A TELEPHONE TOO

And a letterbox. And email. Just get in touch and ask them to be your mentor. Remember, they once asked for someone's help. If you tell them what you are trying to change, and it is important to them too, the chances are they will help you.

Read their books, listens to their talks, read their blogs. They have found a way of making a business out of the thing they love doing. You can learn from them. Suck it all up.

Kevin Spacey was helped at school by the actor Jack Lemmon and told he would make a great actor one day. When Lemmon was asked why he plays small theatres, he replied that it was his duty to send the lift back down to help others.

A great mentor can really help you. Aim high.

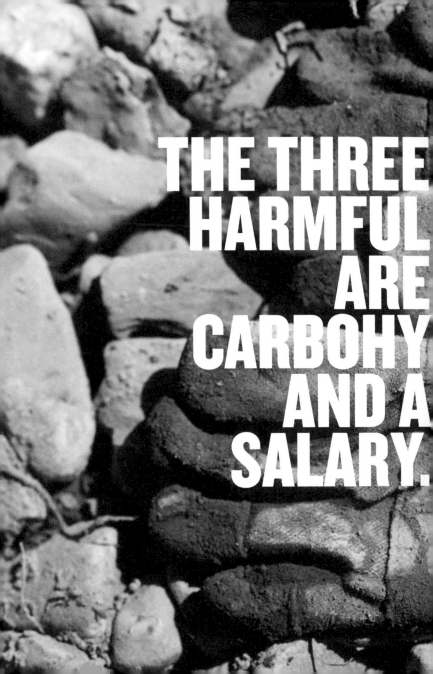

MOST ADDICTIONS HEROIN DRATES MONTHLY

FRED WILSON

WRITE YOUR BUSINESS PLAN ON A DOORMAT

When you order a doormat, they charge per word. This financial restriction makes you think long and hard about what you want to say. The other restriction is that space is limited.

So your thinking needs to be distilled down into the fewest number of words possible. So simple that it can appear on a doormat.

If you could apply the same discipline of writing a doormat to your business plan, I think the chances of you having plenty of customers walking on it would be increased. Why? Because you have no choice but to keep it simple and be clear. And simple and clear are good for business.

So ask yourself what it is that you want to stand for in the fewest number of words that you can:
Kickstarter: *Change Funding of Ideas.*
Patagonia: *Higher Quality. Lower impact.*
Google: *Faster More Relevant Search.*

The less you have to spend on the doormat, the more thinking you have done.

THE BEST BUSINESS MODELS BECOME ROLE MODELS

Look at how Y Combinator has changed startups. Look at how Kickstarter has changed how creative ideas get funded. Look at how ZipCar has changed car ownership. Look at how Welsh Water has changed how a utility can be funded.

These companies become role models for future businesses. Their real influence will be the companies that get started after them. Their business, and their approach to it, will inspire many more businesses to start. They have shown another way. They have been successful. And people follow success.

Their business models will be studied and no doubt applied to other industries. Their books will be purchased, their opinions will be listened to. They have become influential, important and inspiring.

Not many companies can say that.

SPEED MATTERS

DIGITAL WORLD

In the tech world great new companies can be built quickly. They scale big. They scale fast. They scale cheaply. They don't require huge infrastructure. They work best with a small team. They are pioneers. What they are doing has not been done before. They have no map. They are building something fast to get there before their competitor launches. The coder who writes in high-level code is king. Speed matters in this world. How fast you can fix a bug matters. How fast you can add a new feature matters. Patience isn't a virtue here. The need is for speed.

PATIENCE MATTERS

ANALOGUE WORLD

Take an oak tree. It takes 50 years before you get a single acorn. Who'd invest in one of them? Take writers, take artists, take musicians, take inventors, take photographers, take athletes, take any person from any field you can think of, they all took a decade or more to get good at their thing. In those years, learning was put before earning. In those years patience was put before any possible shortcut. We live in a very fast one-click world. Our time to screen in the morning is measured in seconds. Our attention span shrinks with each generation. But building a great analogue company just takes time.

*DON'T RELY ON GOOD
PRINCIPLES TO SELL
A BAD PRODUCT

BUILD SOMETHING YOU WOULD NEVER SELL

Zach Klein gave a talk at the Do Lectures in Wales. He told the story of building Vimeo from nothing. The fun they had. The team they built. The huge following they amassed. Then, one day, they sold it.

The exit strategy is what every startup is geared up for, and yet after selling Vimeo he couldn't help but feel that he missed it. The last slide on his talk summed up his learning from his adventures: Build something that you would never sell.

As a founder of a company, you are going to be faced with this dilemma at some point. So here are some questions to ask yourself before you sell: Do you still love it? Is it still fun? And, is the job only half done? If you answer 'Yes' to these three, my advice would be to keep building.

CHAPTER TWO

TIME

Each day you're given 86,400 seconds from the 'Time Bank'. Everyone is given the same. There are no exceptions. Once you make your withdrawal, you're free to spend it as you want.

The 'Time Bank' won't tell you how to spend it. Time poorly spent will not be replaced with more time. Time doesn't do refunds.

Time is your biggest gift. Indeed, it is more valuable than money as you can make more money, but not more time. But there is one simple truth: Your time is limited. And one day you will go to the bank and it won't have any more for you. And it will be at the exact moment that you will know the answer to this simple question: Did I use my time well?

Did I do what mattered most to me? Did I find my love? And did I pursue it like a wild hungry dog?

ONE

YOUR TIME IS LIMITED. REMEMBER THAT

Treat distractions as the enemy. Luckily, each electrical device you have comes with an off button. Remember, your time is limited. But your ability to be distracted is infinite. If you want to get things done, you have to focus. And focus comes from blocking out that busy world out there.

I am not good at email. But I am good at getting things done. I view email as a distraction from making things happen. I view getting things done as more important than having an empty in-box. I have bought all the apps to help me cope with email. But they don't work for me. It's not them. It's me.

The internet is brilliant but it is one very efficient way of using your time. It's a super-addictive distraction device that will stop us from getting stuff done if we allow it to.

Just click the off button. You got things to do.

TWO

TURN THE INTERNET OFF

There's a point on a runway during take-off that a plane reaches V1 speed. Once it passes V1, it has reached the point of no return. The point where take-off cannot be aborted. It has to take off. Or crash. In order to determine its V1 speed every plane will factor in its weight, wind-speed, weather conditions, slope, length of runway etc. So although there's not a physical line drawn on each runway, it's there.

But when it comes to starting a business, there's no calculation to tell us when the right time is. No marker on a runway for us.

So what happens? We defer. We put barriers up to justify not starting. 'The economy isn't great.' 'I've got a big mortgage.' 'I need more experience.' But as you put those barriers up, only you can tear them down.

There will never be a right time to start. Accept it. So start now.

THREE

BEGIN BEFORE YOU ARE READY

They don't start. The start line is the scariest place. Step beyond it and you can be judged. Step beyond it and you can fail. Step beyond it and you can no longer hide behind what might have been.

Most people talk about starting something one day. But 'one day' doesn't ever come along. They don't get past the start line. Their ideas are probably good enough to succeed. But their belief isn't strong enough.

The patent office doesn't hold the best ideas. They sit in the back of your head waiting for you to believe in them enough to start.

Once you pass that line, you are in the 1% club. Those rare people who turn their ideas into real things. Boom.

FOUR

99% OF BUSINESSES FAIL FOR ONE REASON

If you are given a week to get something done, you will take a week. If you are given two weeks, you will take two weeks. Will the one that took two weeks be twice as good? I doubt it. The first week will have been spent sharpening pencils and tidying the office up. (You know it's true.) The second week will be 'hey, we got to get this down.' So, both projects had a week of your time, if you think about it.

I doubt there will be a discernible difference between the two. Except for the time taken to get them done.

Deadlines rule us. That's how we get stuff done. But deadlines shouldn't be easy. If you want to achieve amazing things quickly, set yourself tough, almost impossible deadlines.

And remember, great coffee helps.

FIVE

SELF-IMPOSED INSANELY IMPOSSIBLE DEADLINES OFTEN HELP

We all want to get as much stuff done as we can, but maybe we are going about it the wrong way.

An experiment in the 1940s measured men loading pig iron onto train freight cars at The Bethlehem Steel Company. Each man didn't stop until they managed 12½ tons. By noon, they were exhausted and could do no more.

The next day, they were told to load the pig iron for 26 minutes. Then rest for 34 minutes. They rested more than they worked. At the end of the day, they had each loaded 47 tons. That's almost 4 times as much as working flat out.

It feels counter-intuitive, but a sprint followed by an even longer rest will deliver better results than plodding along for years.

Yup, the real badge of honour at work is not to work longer than anyone else, but to work smarter than anyone else.

SIX

WANT TO DO MORE? REST UP

THE 80/20 RULE

Pareto's Law is named after an Italian economist Vilfredo Pareto. It is also known as the 80/20 rule, which Richard Koch wrote about in his brilliant book.

The thinking is this: If you run a business, 80% of your business probably comes from 20% of your customers. If you are a creative person, 80% of your awards/recognition/income will come from 20% of your output.

So how can knowing this principle help you manage your time? Well, start by looking at your day. See where you spend most of your time.

The likelihood is you will find out most of your time is spent on the things that you are not that good at. Too many meetings. Too much admin. Too much politics. This is called The Law of Oterap. (Pareto backwards.)

You spend 80% of your time on the things you are least good at. And where you can make the least difference. You don't need more time in the day. You don't need to work longer hours. You don't need to work weekends. You just need to spend more time on what you are brilliant at. And less time on all that other stuff.

BUILDING
A GREAT
COMPANY
JUST
TAKES TIME

IDEAS

How we learn.

How we communicate.

What we eat.

How we play.

How we exercise.

Where we live.

How we travel.

Our behaviour.

Our governments.

Our corporations.

The music we listen to.

How we relax.

How we stay awake.

The status quo.

The perceived wisdom.

'This is how we do
things around here.'

IDEAS
CHANGE
EVERYTHING

SOME IDEAS ARE BORN UGLY

Great ideas often have no reference points.
We have nothing to compare them to. They are
original, and awkward. And so they are the most
vulnerable to people trying to kill them. They do
not conform to what exists, so they challenge us.

So in order to keep the idea alive you will have to
rely on your gut instinct, which sometimes is the
hardest sell of all. You have to believe in it when
no-one else does. The parent has to love the
ugly duckling until it turns into a little beauty.

We also judge ideas too quickly. It's not always
clear from the beginning which are the good,
the bad, and the ugly. Learn not to judge them
too quickly. That dumb idea could be the one.
If you think conventionally you may dismiss the
ugly duckling.

Great ideas cost no more than rubbish ones. That's nice to know. And, if you want to take the stress out of running a business have a great idea.

Ideas don't care about who you are, where you are, they don't go to those with the most money or the biggest smile. They come to you in the bath, in the shower, while going for a run, when you least expect it, and when you need them most. But they will come to you. If you would only just listen. And that's a skill you need to learn. Always be listening.

A great idea will get you more publicity, give you more energy, and will in the end give you more sales. Jake Burton invented a whole new sport: snowboarding. He didn't have a big budget. Just a big idea. A whole new sport.

SMALL BUDGETS REQUIRE BRAVE IDEAS

BE REMARKABLE (PEOPLE DON'T REMEMBER AVERAGE)

How will you stand out when the world rewards mediocrity? The best way is to not play by their rules.

There's a film called *Mystery Train* by Jim Jarmusch. In the film a couple of teenage Elvis fans take the tour of the Graceland Mansion. They walk around in awe. The boy has a camera around his neck for the whole tour, and yet doesn't take a single photo.

When the couple get back to their cheap bedsit, the boy starts taking photos of all the lampshades, the cheap furniture, the bad wallpaper. His girlfriend, slightly surprised, asks him why he is taking photographs of all these dumb things when he hadn't taken a single photo all day long.

He said that he would never forget what he had seen at Graceland Mansion, but all this mundane stuff he would soon forget as it wasn't in any way remarkable. So he was taking photos of it.

IDEAS WORK LIKE VELCRO

Velcro works like this: On one side is a series of hooks going in lots of random directions. On the other side is a series of loops going in lots of random directions. When a hook meets a loop, they connect. It is in the connection business.

It is the randomness of the hooks and the loops that make Velcro work, but they are also important to us if we want to be interesting. We need to have lots of random hooks and loops. If we read the same old books, we get to know more about the thing we know lots about already. We need to subscribe to magazines that we wouldn't normally subscribe to; we need to go to places that we wouldn't normally go to, eat at places that may not be our kind of place.

We stay interesting by stepping outside our groove. We keep pushing; we leave what we know behind for a bit.

This is important from the point of view of coming up with ideas. If your reference points are different to others, then guess what, your ideas are going to be different. To think different: do different, read different, travel different, eat different etc.

Velcro goes in many different directions in order to make a connection. If we are interested in new ideas, so should we.

Inspired by Russell Davies *How to be interesting* Do Course.

HAVE YOUR RADAR ON

How to identify a niche before others? I think that part of your job as an entrepreneur, as a brand builder, is to always have your radar on. When you see someone doing something odd, it's your job to ask, 'What does that mean?' The difference between you and other people is your brain has to think differently. It has to be switched on. It has to notice new behaviours, new patterns, new unanswered needs.

Your eyes and ears will provide most of the answers you will need. You just have to be aware of when they are giving you the answer. To do that your brain has to be switched on. To spot a star, you have to be looking up at the sky and not down at the floor.

So if you want to spot a niche, always be looking. Watch how people use something. Study people. Listen to people when they say, 'I wish someone would...'

SOME IDEAS ARE RIGHT IN FRONT OF YOU

Dietrich Mateschitz went on holiday to Thailand and spotted lots of people drinking a native drink called Krating Daeng. He kept asking himself: 'What does that mean?' His radar was on. He didn't invent Red Bull. It already existed. He just took something he saw on holiday and turned it into a whole new category.

James Dyson wasn't the only person to walk past a sawmill and see the extractor fan at the top. The answer was available to anyone who asked the right question. But he was the only one to go and make vacuum cleaners using that technology. Yes, it took him five years and over 5,000 iterations. He didn't invent the idea. He took an idea from another industry and applied it to vacuum cleaners. He made it work.

A lot of times the ideas are there right in front of you just waiting for you to take that idea and put it into another industry or country.

THE FORMULA FOR CHANGE
$D \times V \times F > R$

There may not be a formula for ideas, but there is a formula for change. It was created by Richard Beckhard and David Gleicher. The formula provides a model to assess the relative strengths affecting the likely success of a project.

Three factors must be present for meaningful organisational change to take place.
These factors are:

D = Dissatisfaction with how things are now.
V = Vision of what is possible.
F = First, concrete steps that can be taken towards the vision.

If the product of these three factors is greater than R = Resistance then change is possible.

Because D, V, and F are multiplied, if any one is absent or low, then the product will be low and therefore not capable of overcoming the resistance.

It's easy to become comfortable. It's easy to stop pushing. It's easy to do what you did last year. It worked, for goodness' sake.

It is harder to question everything. To walk in dumb each day. To start again with a blank piece of paper.

There is a difference between companies who are always thinking about new ways forward. And those who seek to repeat themselves.

Those who repeat themselves have an easy life, then one day they wake up and their business is no longer there. The easy life is replaced with a hard life.

Those who keep pushing never have an easy life. They never get to freewheel downhill. They keep cycling like crazy because it is a good mindset for when the hills come. That way of thinking means you never wake up to find the business gone, either.

Tomorrow the reputation has to be made again.

DON'T FREEWHEEL

FALLOW

FAILURE TO COMMIT IS AS BAD AS FAILURE TO START

Ideas need someone to make them happen. Ideas need doers not talkers. Ideas require your total belief in them. So before you cross that line, just make sure you are 100% into it. Businesses can fail for many reasons.

Perhaps the founders don't quite believe in the idea, or one of the partners loses his or her nerve when the first test comes at them.

A lack of belief can be much more damaging than a lack of funding.

In Football terms, this is the equivalent of not fully committing in the tackle. And when you are half-hearted in the tackle, you are much more likely to get injured.

Players who are saving themselves for the next big game or an important tournament often end up injured because they held back. Holding back often ends in tears.

Likewise, ideas need you to commit. They need all your money. They need all your time. They need all your energy. They need all your love. They need all your belief. If you are half-hearted about the idea, don't even start.

IF YOU'RE GOING TO TRY, GO ALL THE WAY. OTHERWISE, DON'T EVEN START.

1   Is it a good idea?
2   Is it a new idea?
3   Is it scalable?
4   Will people want it?
5   What change will it bring about?
6   Is it investable?
7   Does it matter to you?
8   Does it matter to your customer?
9   How do you know?
10 How big is the change it can make?
11 Is it good for the planet?
12 Is it good for the human?
13 What is your niche?
14 How big is that niche?
15 How will you test it?
16 Is it a common problem?
17 Ask yourself, does this problem need solving?
18 What disruption will it bring?
19 Where will it be in five years' time?
20 Do you love it?
21 Would you spend ten years doing it?
22 What will its legacy be?
23 If you are uncertain about your idea now, keep going.

23 QUESTIONS TO ASK OF YOUR IDEA

CHAPTER FOUR

BRAND

Have you noticed that you have more ideas when you are not thinking about the thing you should be thinking ab... Umm...

THE CREATORS CODE

1 Find your love.
2 Spend your life at it.
3 Trust your instincts.
4 Ignore doubters.
5 Chase the work, not the money.
   (The money will come.)
6 Use your ideas to push this world forward.
7 Don't let your ideas down: Execute well.
8 Work with great people. They are not always
   the easiest.
9 There are no shortcuts. Do the hours.
10 Great coffee helps.

Some people think once they have a name and a logo for their company, they have a brand. What they have at that point is just a name and a logo. No more.

The job of the brand is to make that name and that logo stand for something. To live its founding principles each day. To stay true. How do you do that? Well, by making a great product, giving a great service, and by using your company as the tool to change the things that you said you would. It's not difficult. Just hard.

Of course, a good name and a good logo help. But do you think Apple would have made it if they were called Peach? Of course, they would have.

I think of a brand as consistent promise. 'I promise to make the best running shoes on the planet', 'I promise to provide faster more relevant search', 'I promise to make the highest quality outdoor clothing with the least amount of harm to the planet'. What's your promise? Your promise is your brand.

A BRAND ISN'T JUST A NICE LOGO

HOW TO GET PEOPLE TO LOVE YOUR BRAND

I get asked this a lot. And there is a surprisingly simple answer: You have to love it the most first. That's it? Yeah, that's it.

This is a 'Labour of Love'. And you're the 'Labour' they are referring to. You have to sweat each detail. Over and over again. Relentlessly paying obsessive attention to the littlest tiny weeny bit. And guess what, your customers will notice. They will see that you have poured your heart into it, and they will love that you care that much about them.

At every stage you will have put the customer first. Always. Don't let bean counters cut quality in order to improve margins. Long-term relationships with your customers should never be sacrificed for short-term profits. It is much easier to find a new bean counter than find a new customer.

The customer can tell when a company loves its customers. And that love is felt and appreciated. Love scales.

This is a story I was told about Ralph Lauren.
It may, or may not, be true.

Anyway, the story goes like this. He spent
millions building his ranch. Every detail
considered. The builders and the architects had
a tough old time of it. It was redone a couple
of times. After it was finally finished, they were
super happy. But, for Ralph, something was
missing. Something wasn't quite right. The
builders had to come back because the door
was too perfect. It didn't squeak. And everyone
knows old ranches always have a squeaky door.
So they had to put one in.

Imagine how much detail is considered for
his clothes.

A brand is about consistency. Each detail paid
attention to. Because consistency builds trust.
And trust builds a business. And, as the founder,
it is your job to be the guardian of these details.
What matters? Only everything.

THE ONLY THING THAT MATTERS IS EVERYTHING

REPUTATIONS TAKE DECADES TO MAKE. AND ONE WASH TO LOSE

The first clothing company I started had made a reputation for making excellent merino base layers. The margin wasn't the best, but we never had to go to sale. We couldn't get enough of it. But a buyer had seen the margin – and wanted to improve it.

Their way of improving it was to buy an inferior quality grade of merino. It was, of course, a better margin. We all tried it. And it was simply not good enough. The merino became saggy after just one wash. As soon as I saw this, I stopped it. But the buyer couldn't understand it. The buyer even tried to bypass me in order to purchase behind my back. I stopped that too.

For me, there is no point achieving a great margin once, only to lose that customer after one wash. Your brand reputation should never be compromised for a short-term gain.

YOUR VOICE CAN BE MANY THINGS

I sat down for a coffee with Richard, one of the founders of innocent, and he told me his taxi story. He was taking a ride back to work I think. Anyway, as all taxi drivers do, he wanted to make conversation. His went along normal lines. What do you do, mate? Richard replied, I help run a smoothie company. Oh yeah, which one? Innocent. Nice company. But it's not the same any more. Richard was a bit taken aback. How do you mean? Well, you changed the label. It's glossy now and the other one was matt. So it doesn't feel as real any more, you know as authentic. Richard thanked him once he was dropped off. And he went inside work and the first thing he did was change the label back from glossy to matt.

The taxi driver had just taught him the importance of the bigness of small. How those little things that we don't think are that important have a huge impact. If you want to build something big, do all the small things right.

HOW MANY SENSES DOES YOUR BRAND USE?

A brand should appeal to all your senses. But most brands only appeal to sight and sound. They leave touch, smell and taste alone. And yet they can be very powerful. Abercrombie and Fitch spray each catalogue with their perfume: it acts as a reminder when you walk into the stores. Jawbone, the portable speakers, sound like a futuristic space ship taking off when you switch one on. If you want convincing that they are state of the art technology, just turn it on. It is quite something.

The chef Ferran Adrià believes that taste is not the only sense to appeal to, which is interesting. Touch can be played with through various temperatures, as can smell and sight. To him the senses become one of the main points of reference in the creative process.

It isn't just coffee shops that can tap the power of the sense of smell. It isn't just chefs who can tap the power of the sense of taste. And it isn't just clothing companies who can tap into the power of the sense of touch. Is your brand using all our senses?

MAKE THEM FEEL SOMETHING FOR THE CHANGE YOU'RE MAKING

The best brands not only change something, they also have a great innate ability to communicate their purpose well, so it matters to their customers.

You have to make your customers feel something for the change you are making, or you will change very little. Understand what is in their hearts. Logic is a blunt tool in this regard. It makes perfect sense, it ticks all the boxes, but it changes very little. And guess what, intelligence is no better; it is overrated in its ability to either change things or behaviour. I think one of the best ways to leave your customers inspired, stirred, awoken, is to use emotion. Make them feel something.

Bare your soul. Tell your struggle. Tell your pain. Tell your lows. Be vulnerable. Be honest. Tell them how the world could be.

But most of all, be you.

YOUR VOICE
BE CONSISTENT WITH IT

A worthwhile business has to be built over time. A company's product, its purpose and how it speaks to the world needs to be consistent if it wants to be everything that it hopes to be.

So do not blow with the wind. Do not chase a bandwagon. Stay true. Patience is required in a world that doesn't always understand the value of it. It is easy to make little changes in a busy day and think they do not matter. But there is a big-ness to small decisions.

The financial world fully understands the concept of compound interest and how a small change can make a big difference. Similarly, a small tweak here, a small compromise there, can accumulate over time to change the very soul of a business.

The rule of consistent product and service are understood by everyone. But the same rule needs to be applied to a company's voice. Nike has talked with the same voice for a couple of decades now. A signature seems to run through it.* And because it is so consistent, each communication seems to build on top of the last one. They have gained compound interest of voice thanks to their consistency of voice.

*Nike owe Wieden and Kennedy a little something.

YOUR STORY. TELL IT WELL

A brand is a story. And you have to tell it well. The good news in this connected world is great stories travel fast. And, these days, they travel for free. So there has never been a better time or a cheaper time to start something. Big companies no longer have a huge advantage. Your website can make you look as big as them. Your Instagrams can make you funnier than them, your Tweets can make you look more human than them.

The tools at your disposal are very powerful, and very free. Tools like: Medium (free), Stumble Upon (free), Instagram (free), Twitter (free). Digital cameras, they get cheaper with each season.

Your ability to make a great unique product will need to be matched by your ability to tell your story. Don't take a quick picture, take a considered one, don't write an OK blog, spend days writing a great one, don't make a film that is good when a great one just takes a little more sweat.

Do the work.
Tell your story well.

We live in a very busy world. We have the same amount of time as before, but there are so many more things competing for our attention. What gets it? The things that stand out. Average sinks to the bottom. Fast.

Average viral films don't get shared. Average Instagrams don't get liked. Boring tweets don't get re-tweeted. Social media takes no prisoners. It's binary. You either have our attention. Or not. It's ruthless in sorting out the good from the bad.

The good thing is this: Excellent costs no more than average. In fact, you can argue that average costs more than excellent. All the money and effort to make something that no one is going to see is a dumb waste of money. The answer is to spend more time on being creative. It will pay you back in spades.

AVERAGE DIES FASTER THAN EVER BEFORE

Ever been to a great restaurant where the waiter was just plain not interested? Ever been in a famous shop when the sales person chatted to their mates on the phone for your entire time in the shop? Ever been to a 5-star hotel and the service was darned awful? It doesn't matter who you are, if you hire people who don't care, they will do their very best to reveal it to your customers.

And all that work you have put in gets crushed. So when you hire, ask yourself this: Are they passionate about what you are about? Are they a good fit with your brand and its principles? When you walk in through the door at Abercrombie and Fitch, it soon becomes very clear what is on brand for them.

Who you hire will represent you when you are not there. Does that frighten you or comfort you?

YOUR PEOPLE ARE YOUR BRAND

CHAPTER FIVE

PEOPLE

TEAMS
GATHER
AROUND
CHANGE

Your purpose will define your product. The culture of your company. The people you hire. Even your customers who buy from you. And ultimately it will define how successful you are. But perhaps the most important thing that your purpose gives everyone in the company is a clear understanding of why the company exists. Everyone in the company understands what it is that you are going to change.

Change is your secret fuel. People want to be part of change. People want to be part of history. Teams gather around ideas that will change things.

That's why your purpose matters. It builds teams who are passionate about the project. They are there to make a difference, not just to make a quick buck.

When a team is motivated, when a team understands the change it will make, even when the odds are stacked against it, it is an impossible thing to stop.

TEAMS BUILD
A BUSINESS.
CULTURE
BUILDS
A TEAM

A company is only as strong as the people that work in it. The people are only as strong as the culture that exists within the company. And the purpose of the company, its reason to exist, will define the culture.

Culture is a funny thing to talk about. You can't see it. You can't feel it. But when it's not right, you can both see it and feel it. Culture is not a big thing. Just lots of small things.

Patagonia let their people go surfing when the surf is good. At my Hiut Denim Co, every pair of jeans is signed by the GrandMasters who made them: All artists sign their work. At Nike, it created a group called the Ekins. They know Nike backwards. Some even had a tattoo to show they were part of the elite.

When you define your purpose, it attracts like-minded people as a moth is attracted to light. So define it well.

Your culture will attract your people. Nike started life as a running company. It was founded by a runner and a running coach. Its first employee was Jeff Johnson. He was a runner too. That was its culture. They wanted to change running.

Johnson created the first product brochures, print ads and marketing materials, and even shot the photographs for the company's catalogues. He established a mail-order system, opened the first store. He also designed several early Nike shoes, and even conjured up the name Nike in 1971.

Even more than doing all this, he wrote letters to athletes to see how things were going with training. When it came to the Olympics and they had to choose between wearing Adidas or Nike, they chose the one who had taken an interest in their running. Those letters changed Nike's history.

Who is going to be your first hire?

EMPLOYEE NUMBER 1

HIRE SLOWLY

Make the interview last longer. An hour is not enough. You will get to know more about them by setting them a live project. Give them a short deadline. See how they get on. It will tell you so much more than an interview* ever will.

Take them out of the office. Go for a run with them. Have a beer with them. See them as people. If you can't spend time with them, do you really want to hire them?

Remember, a crazy amount of your management time will be spent on a wrong hire. A lot of your stress will come from having to deal with a wrong hire. So can you afford to spend more of your time on making the hiring process longer? Yup, I think so.

*Introverts don't interview well, but can have the best ideas.

FIRE QUICKLY

Not every hire works out. And both parties know it quickly. Within three months you know that, well, it isn't going to end well. And yet companies don't act. The person isn't happy. The team isn't happy.* And that can last for years. Decades, even.

Your duty is to the team, the culture, and ultimately to the purpose of the company. And, therefore, you have to do the difficult thing quickly.

The person would be happier in another job. The team would be happier with another person. And life is too short for people to be miserable. People make the mistake of being nice, and not dealing with the problem. This means the person is unhappier for longer. It may seem counter-intuitive, but there is a kindness to acting quickly.

*A players prefer to be around A players.

NO ARSEHOLE RULE

One way to break a team is to hire someone who is talented, but will destroy the team spirit. Because of their talent they have been indulged in other companies. They have been allowed to be monsters. They are out for themselves. And they will do anything they can to win. But the one thing they won't do is to put the team first.

We have all played football with a talented player who can do everything with the ball at his feet but pass it to his team mates. He may score a great goal, but the team will lose the game.

A good friend told me the story of seven matchsticks. How each one on its own could be snapped. But when you join them together, no one can break them. The most talented people know they can't do it alone. Teams win.

HIRE HUNGER
OVER TALENT

In an ideal world you would have both these things in one person. Alas, that isn't always possible. So if you had to choose, I would choose Hunger.

Hunger is always keen to learn. Always trying to get better. Hunger is always putting the extra hours in. Hunger doesn't get lazy.

Over time Hunger works so hard at his thing that his Talent begins to shine above even someone with a natural gift for it. Hunger is normally insecure about his Talent. So continues to work at it. He never loses the Hunger. So just keeps putting the practice in. Malcolm Gladwell believes 'Talent is the desire to practise'. I am pretty sure he is right on that.

Indeed Talent comes from the hunger to get better. You can't give people hunger. You can't train it or inspire it. They either have it in their belly or not. It comes with them when they walk in the room. Or not.

I agree with the Real Madrid chairman: Expensive is cheap. His point is that buying a £70 million player was better value than buying a £10 million player. The Galacticos (as he calls them) sold more shirts, got more press and did more for the 'Real Madrid' brand around the world. The £10 million players did none of these things, so he deemed them expensive.

I am figuring you don't have £70 million to burn on talent. But if you want to succeed, you will have to work with the best.

So whether it's a website builder, a photographer, a designer, a hacker, tell them your small budget means they can have creative freedom. The one thing creative people want is to show the rest of the world how creative they are. So you can't give them lots of money, but you can give them lots of freedom. Let them fly. They live to fly.

WORK WITH THE BEST

ESPECIALLY IF YOU'RE AN UNDER-FUNDED STARTUP

BUILD A VIRTUAL TEAM

In Startup mode you can't hire all the team you want from day one. But you know who they are, right? You've been admiring their work for years.

So how can you get them on the team? Write to them. Show them pictures of their work in your scrapbook. And tell them your mission. And tell them the change you will make.

Recently I was working with our graphic designer Nick Hand (Virtual Team Member) on the Yearbook for Hiut Denim Co. He came in with a book from a famous graphic designer and illustrator in New York (James Victore). I loved his work. His work was already in my scrapbooks. 'We need to work with people as good as him,' said Nick.

I was thinking, we don't need to work with people like him. We need to work *with* him. So somehow I found out his email. And I wrote to him. I told him my town was going to make jeans again. And if we wanted to get everybody their jobs back we would have to be brilliant. And that meant we could only work with the best. So we had to work with him. He wrote back and said 'I'm in'.* If I had looked at our budget, I would never have sent him the email.

*He also designed the cover for this book.

MAKE YOUR COMPANY A PLACE TO LEARN

People don't leave companies for money.
They say they do. But they don't.

They leave emotionally long before they leave
physically. They leave because they are not
valued, they are not being challenged or feel
part of something that matters to them. A
central plank to all this discontent is they have
stopped learning.

It's your job to create a learning culture that will
keep them emotionally connected. You have to
keep their hearts in the business. Training is the
best way I know to do that.

And it isn't just training to do their job better.
That's standard stuff. But you will need to go
beyond that to get people engaged.

You will need to send them on courses, even
if that course is unrelated to what they do
with you. The best companies see the whole
person, and not just the little segment that
they do for you.

THE ONLY THING
WORSE THAN
TRAINING YOUR
EMPLOYEES
AND HAVING
THEM LEAVE
IS NOT
TRAINING THEM
AND HAVING
THEM STAY.
HENRY FORD

TRUST

Tina Roth Eisenberg (better known as @swissmiss) gave a talk at Do USA. She talked a lot about building her amazing companies, and building the team, and the importance of fun. One of the slides that she put up read: Trust breeds **magic**.

Yup, like Tina, I believe in teams. I believe when a team comes together, there is very little that they can't do. But some teams end up fighting each other like crazy, and subsequently, they go the way of the dinosaur. This fascinates me. So why do some teams come together, and others fall apart?

I know, in order to build a business, I have to build a team first. It is one of the key skills that an entrepreneur has to learn.

BREEDS

Building a team isn't complex. My learning is that a team is galvanised by two things. Firstly, they like to gather around the founding idea of the company. The more that idea is going to change things, the more people will want to gather around it. Purpose is important.

The second thing teams love to gather around is a leader they trust. Trust is a multiplier of energy for a team. In order for the team to trust the leader, the leader has to show the team that he or she trusts them. Trust is a two-way street.

But most companies are not set up to trust their people. In fact, they are set up to do the opposite. And yet trust is free. It breeds loyalty, passion and helps us all pull together. The magic of trust is that it helps a team to become a team.

CHAPTER SIX

YOU

PLAY THE LONG GAME

The problem with a purpose-driven company is that it matters to you.

And, oh boy, it can and will consume you. Every waking hour. Every sleeping hour. At home. At work. And the journey between the two.

That's the deal. But you have to find ways to look after yourself. Because you look after lots of other people, who depend on you.

Accept that working through the night is a rite of passage, and working weekends goes with the territory. But also accept that these can't become the norm.

Tired? Go home. Come in fresh. Businesses are very good at running you. Don't let it.

SLEEP IS THE MULTIPLIER OF ENERGY

Great businesses are built on huge amounts of energy. Even more important than huge amounts of funding.

You can burn the candle at both ends for a while, but there comes a point where you get diminishing returns.

You job is to lead. Your job is to make decisions. Your job is to be a bundle of energy and enthusiasm.

It may sound boring, but if you are going to give your company its best chance of success, you need to get the amount of sleep that your body requires. There is no badge of honour for who is the most tired.

IF YOU WANT A GUARANTEE, BUY A TOASTER

Some advice: If you worry a lot, starting a business may not be for you. It doesn't come with a guarantee. Things rarely go as per business plan. And each day comes with a new challenge.

So what are the tricks to stop worrying?

Firstly, write down on a plain piece of paper 'what is the worst that can possibly happen?' Is it that I will lose this house? Is it loss of reputation? Is it fear of failure? And accept that before you start. If you can't accept it, don't start.

READ
THIS
BOOK

Dale Carnegie wrote a book all about how to deal with worry. He noticed businessmen were dying of stress-related illnesses. He did some research in his local library. There were 47 books on worms. And just one on worry. That made him worry so much, he went and wrote a book all about it.

It may have been written a half a century ago, but it has some nuggets of gold amongst its pages. Before you set off and start your thing, give yourself some techniques to help you cope with worry. Businesses are very good at running you.

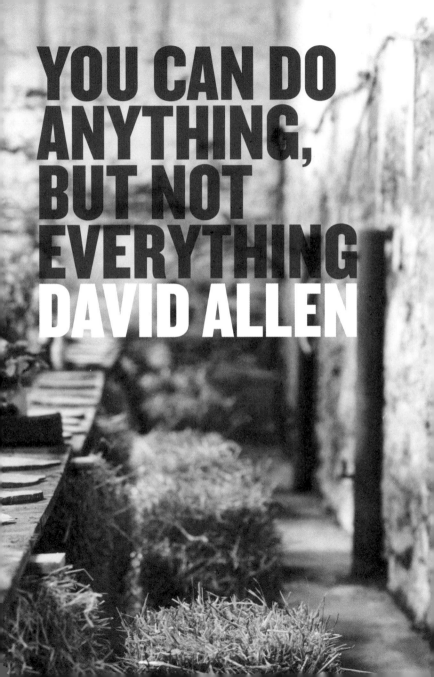

YOU CAN DO ANYTHING, BUT NOT EVERYTHING

DAVID ALLEN

FIND
ANOTHER
DISTRACTION

Lots of people who run a business find it hard to switch off. That is because they are obsessive control freaks. Nothing wrong with that, by the way.

One way to switch off is to find something else to obsess over. Take up a sport or get a hobby and obsess over that. Take up golf, fishing, yoga, tool making, baking bread etc.

While you're obsessing over your hobby, you can take your mind off the business – it may give you ideas that will help you. Sometimes the best way to have ideas is to be thinking of something else.

Sport is important. Whatever you do, take time out. Whether it's a run, a walk, a bike ride, or daily meditation.

The brain needs some rest. Work the body, and while the body is so busy doing its stuff, the brain switches off.

You feel fresher physically and mentally. Feel the burn of sport. There are no emails to send, no bills to pay, no awkward people conversations. You are free*.

Sport takes the stress of the day away and leaves it far behind.

* And free is a good place to go to as often as you can.

LIFE IS COMPLICATED. BUT SPORT IS SIMPLE

**NATURE
LIKES
BALANCE**

And so do the bodies and minds that work for you. When you are involved in a startup, life can quickly go out of control. If you allow it to. Yes, there will be times when a deadline means burning the midnight oil. And yes, adrenaline is the fuel of startups but mostly because it is cheap. But not because it is the best fuel to build a long-term business.

So your job is to look after the team because they look after the business. So you have to make sure that those crazy times do not become the norm. You have to create a culture where people take their holidays, where late nights are the exception, where people eat well, sleep well, and use their time well. (Read David Allen's *Getting Things Done* book. It is a secret weapon.)

Your team are more creative, think better, and much more fun to be around too, if you can create a culture of balance.

DO ONE THING WELL

IT'S ENOUGH.

ENJOY THE RIDE, IT'S YOUR RIDE

Deal with each day one day at a time. Don't dwell on the past. Don't live in the future. Keep working in the now. Head down. Working on the thing that matters to you. Stay in the now.

Don't spend your time moaning. Be thankful for each day. And enjoy the ride. It's your ride. You are making the decisions. Get your mind looking for the positives and not the negatives. Surround yourself with people who take you up and not bring you down.

Even the hardest days you will have, you will look back on with a smile.

Books

Purpose

Let My People Go Surfing: The
Education of a Reluctant Businessman
Yvon Chouinard (Penguin, 2006)

Start with Why: How Great Leaders
Inspire Everyone to Take Action
Simon Sinek (Penguin, 2011)

Small Giants: Companies That
Choose to be Great Instead of Big
Bo Burlingham (Penguin, 2007)

Brand

The Republic of Tea: The Story of
the Creation of a Business, as
Told Through the Personal Letters
of Its Founders
Mel Ziegler, Patricia Ziegler,
Bill Rosenzweig (Crown,
Random House 1994)

Steve Jobs: The Exclusive Biography
Walter Isaacson (Little Brown, 2011)

It's Not How Good You Are, It's
How Good You Want To Be
Paul Arden (Phaidon, 2003)

Winning the Story Wars: Why Those
Who Tell and Live the Best Stories
Will Rule the Future
Jonah Sachs (Harvard, 2012)

Product

The Lean Startup
Eric Ries (Crown,
Random House, 2011)

The Synergist: How to Lead Your
Team to Predictable Success
Les McKeown
(Palgrave MacMillan, 2012)

Hackers & Painters: Big Ideas from
the Computer Age
Paul Graham (O'Reilly, 2004)

Time

Getting Things Done: How to
Achieve Stress-free Productivity
David Allen (Piatkus, 2002)

The 80/20 Principle: The Secret
of Achieving More with Less
Richard Koch (Nicholas Brealey
Publishing, 2007)

The 4-Hour Work Week,
Timothy Ferriss (Vermilion,
Random House, 2011)

People

Leaders Eat Last: Why Some Teams
Pull Together and Others Don't
Simon Sinek (Portfolio Penguin, 2014)

Books

The Score Takes Care of Itself:
My Philosophy of Leadership
Bill Walsh (Portfolio Penguin, 2010)

Turn the Ship Around!: A True Story
of Building Leaders by Breaking
the Rules
L David Marquet
(Portfolio Penguin, 2013)

Wooden on Leadership: How to
Create a Winning Organization
John Wooden (McGraw-Hill, 2005)

Who Moved My Cheese: An
Amazing Way to Deal with Change
in Your Work and in Your Life
Spencer Johnson (Vermilion,
Random House, 1999)

Ideas

Insanely Simple: The Obsession
That Drives Apple's Success
Ken Segall (Portfolio Penguin, 2012)

A Technique for Producing Ideas
James W Young (Frontal Lobe
Publishing, 2011)

The War of Art: Break Through
the Blocks and Win Your Inner
Creative Battles
Steven Pressfield (Black Irish
Entertainment, 2012)

The Tao of Warren Buffett:
Warren Buffett's Words of Wisdom
Mary Buffet & David Clark
(Pocket Books, 2009)

You

How To Stop Worrying
And Start Living
Dale Carnegie (Vermilion, Random
House, 1993. First published 1948)

Turning Pro: Tap Your Inner Power
and Create Your Life's Work
Steven Pressfield (Black Irish
Entertainment, 2012)

Clarity: Clear Mind, Better
Performance, Bigger Results
Jamie Smart (Capstone, 2013)

The Power of Less: The 6 Essential
Productivity Principels That Will
Change Your Life
Leo Babauta (Hay House, 2009)

The Little Prince
Antoine De Saint-Exupery
(First published 1943)

Zen Mind, Beginner's Mind: Informal
Talks on Zen Meditation and Practice,
Shunryu Suzuki (Shambhala, 2005.
First published 1970)

Other resources

Quotes

'Trust Breeds Magic.'
Tina Roth Eisenberg, aka SwissMiss

'You can't get to wonderful without
passing through alright.'
Bill Withers

'The three most harmful addictions
are heroin, carbohydrates, and a
monthly salary.'
Fred Wilson

'You can do anything,
but not everything.'
David Allen

'The more classic you can make
something, the longer it will last.'
Paul Arden

'Chase the work, and not the money.
And the money will come.'
Paul Arden

'Be regular and orderly in your life, so
that you may be violent and original in
your work.'
Gustave Flaubert

'Efficiency only matters if you don't
like what you're doing.'
Adam Shand
on building his own house

'The biggest investment you can make
is in yourself not a house. '
Warren Buffet

'The danger for most of us is not that
our aim is too high and we miss it,
but that it is too low and we reach it '
Michelangelo

Websites

thedolectures.com

99u.com

creativemornings.com

paulgraham.com

thesummit.co

scrapbookchronicles.hiutdenim.co.uk

thecleanestline.com

ted.com

About the author

David Hieatt has been described as a marketing genius. After leaving Saatchi and Saatchi, he built howies into one of the most influential active sports brands of the last decade. After selling it to Timberland, he co-founded The Do Lectures. It was voted in the top ten ideas festivals in the world by The Guardian and now takes place in West Wales, California and Australia. More recently he started Hiut Denim in his home town of Cardigan. A town that used to have Britain's biggest jeans factory. Hiut Denim's purpose is to get 400 people their jobs back. David has spoken at Apple, Google, and many other top companies. In 2010 he self-published *The Path of a Doer*.

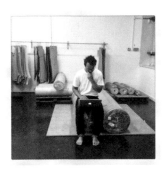

The author and publisher are grateful to the following readers who pledged their support and made this book happen via the crowdfunding platform, Unbound. If you'd like to join them, visit: www.unbound.co.uk.

Tom Abba
Phil Adams
Marcus Ainley
Jon Akass
Elizabeth Kairys Allspaw
Jeff Alpen
Mishaal AlQurashi
Rob Amour
Andy Annett
Steve Ardagh
Lorne Armstrong
Helen Arney
Andrew Arnold
Alicia Artiaga
James Axtell
Tom Baldwin
Iancu Barbarasa
Martin Bavio
Graham Beanlands
Richard & Mimi Beaven
Samantha Bell
Steven Bennett-Day
Sarah Benton
Andrew Beverley
Jon Boaden
James Boardwell
Clara Boland
Nick Bolton
Sheila Bounford
Justin Bovington
Stuart Bowdler
Lisa Bowen
Julie Bozza
Toby Bray
Kim Bremer
Nic Brisbourne
Jayne Bromfield
Dan Burgess
Liam Burgess
Markus Busch
Alex Butler
Stuart Butler
Jerome Camblain
Beth Cwtch Camp
Sarah Mac Cann
Xander Cansell

canteen canteen
David Carroll
Mark Carroll
Matthew Chamberlain
Hinching Chan
Juliet Chen
Sean Pillot de Chenecey
Andy & Lauren Clark
Toby Clark
Richard Clarke
Roxanne Coady
Sandy Coffey
Deborah Colella
Ben Coleman
Stevyn Colgan
James Cooper
Sarah Corbett
Mike Coulter
Ed Cowburn
Bella Cranmore
Ian Crocombe
Daniel Crowell
David Cummings
Tom Darlington
Ben Davies
DCA Consultants
Jack and Maggie Dean
Elizabeth DeLana
Andy Dennis
Kevin Donnellon
Julie Donovan
Jillian Dougan
James Downes
Mark Durbin
Tim Edwards
Simon Edwards
Tina Roth Eisenberg
Aidan Ellis
Ben Emmens
Cyriel van 't End
Graham, Bertha's Pizza
Paul Farmiga
Christoph Faschian
Chinyere Feasey
Patrick Filbee
Mark Foster

Luke Francis
Mark Franich
Tim Frenneaux
Jamie Fries
Mariken Gaanderse
Hilary Gallo
Carl Gaywood
Bobby George
Adam Gill
Guy Gillon
GJD
Salena Godden
Gary Goodson
Chris Goor
Pete Gosnell
Jon Grafflin
John Grant
Stephen Green
Paul Greer
Iwan Griffiths
Andrew Hale
Susan Harper
Andrew Harrison
Cornel Hess
Ross Hill
Matthew Hinchliffe
Stuart Hobday &
Stephanie Lynn
Nick Honey
Richard Horne
Jo Howard
John Howe
Daniel Howell
Rich Howell
Alastair Humphreys
Matt Hunt
Zach Inglis
Jodie Inkson
Scott James
Mark Jenkins
Giles Jepson
Bernadette Jiwa
Andy Johns
Mark Johnson
Damion Jones
Barry Jordan

Matthew Judkins
George Julian
Vincent Kamp
Rebecca Kaye
Hilary Kemp
Al Kennedy
Jonathan Kennedy
Jake Kenny
Andy Kent
Dan Kieran
Stephen King
Sarah King
Emma Klose
Andrew Kluge
Lisajane Koea
Jörg Kreß
Carl Laidler
Adrian Lake
Matt Lane
Tom Lawton
Jimmy Leach
Jonny Lennon
Rich Lennon
Alex Lewis
Anthony Lewis
Beth Lewis
Anthony Lewis
Simon Lilly
Sue Llewellyn
Hywel Lloyd
Lloydie Lloyd
Jerry Lockspeiser
Craig Lockwood
Lost in the Forest Institute
Isaac Lowe
Kuan Luo
Pierre Minik Lynge
Ross MacDonald
Rob Malvisi
Johnny Martin
Thomas McConaghie
Andrew Mckee
Les McKeown
Eddie McMullan
James McQuarrie
Chris Mead

Sian Meadowcroft
Sascha Mengerink
Ann Menke
Andy Middleton
Lee Middleton
Rob Miles
John Mitchinson
Vicky Morley
Jennifer Nash
Sarah Newton
Matt Nicholls
Andrew Nicholson
Mike Nicholson
Par Olsson
Anthony Oram
Martin Orton
Avalon Paravicini
David Parker
Andrew Parkes
Nick Pennell
Jonny Philp
Catherine Pickersgill
Alexia Pinchbeck
Kevin Points
Gordon Pollard
Justin Pollard
Gary Pyke
Taff Ramsey
Amaya Darcy Ritson
Eric Roberts
Tom Roberts
Sally Rosenthal
Charles Ross
Laurie Roth
Christopher Ruane
Mary Rush
Rachel Rutter
Karine Sabatier
Claire Sambrook
Christoph Sander
Andre Santos
Jonathan Satchell
Richard Seabrooke
Sean Sharp
Paul Smith
Christopher Smith

Sam Smith
Alisdair and Amanda Smyth
Barry Smyth
Matt Spry
Benedict Steele
Cameron Stewart
Jon Stewart
Mari Stølan
Gordon Stovin
SuperNatural Collections
Chris Sweetman
Patrick Tanguay
Jono Taylor
Mike Teasdale
Simon Terry
Chris Thomas
Piers Thomas
Nicholas Tomlinson
Robert Turrall
Simon Ü
Roderic Vincent
Patrick Walker
Linda Wanstreet
Graeme Ward
Rebecca Ward
Jonathan Waring
Adam Washington
Richard Watson
Tanya Weaver
Richard Webber
Martin Weber
Mike Weiss
Chris Welton
Miranda West
The Weston's of Worcester
Austin White
Max White
Gary Whiteley
(Maesyffin Mushrooms)
Janet Wilkinson
Adam Williams
Michael Townsend Williams
Jacky Williamson
Arjan van Woensel
Woodsman Bicycle Company
Ben Young

Books in the series:

Do Birth
A gentle guide to labour and childbirth
Caroline Flint

Do Disrupt
Change the status quo. Or become it
Mark Shayler

Do Grow
Start with 10 simple vegetables
Alice Holden

Do Improvise
Less push. More Pause. Better results
A new approach to work (and life)
Robert Poynton

Do Lead
Share your vision. Inspire others.
Achieve the impossible
Les McKeown

Do Protect
Legal advice for startups
Johnathan Rees

Do Purpose
Why brands with a purpose do better
and matter more
David Hieatt

Do Sourdough
Slow bread for busy lives
Andrew Whitley

Do Story
How to tell your story so the world listens
Bobette Buster

Available in print and digital formats
from bookshops, online retailers
or via our website:
thedobook.co

To hear about events and
forthcoming titles, you can find us on
Twitter @dobookco, Facebook
or subscribe to our online newsletter.